What About Me?

By William G. Bentrim

**Bearly
Tolerable
Publications**

bearlytolerablepub@bentrim.info

Acknowledgements:

Kudos to my wife for her editing and patience.

Author's Note

A sick or injured child can disrupt the best of families. Parents are frequently so focused on the sick child that well siblings may feel abandoned. In spite of the love they feel for their sibling, a well child may be annoyed with all the attention their sick sibling receives. The well child may feel guilty about their anger or annoyance. Conflicting emotions can overwhelm the healthiest child. This book hopes to demonstrate to the healthy child that their feelings are normal, acceptable and guilt is not necessary. The book also hopes to alleviate any of the well child's feelings of alienation and loneliness by reassuring them of their parents love.

Bradley was depressed. Ever since Bonnie fell off the swing and broke her leg, things had been bad. He felt like he had a dark cloud over his head all of the time.

Bradley was angry too. Everybody was saying, poor Bonnie this and poor Bonnie that. Bonnie was getting cards, toys and phone calls from aunts and uncles. They were all saying poor Bonnie. What about me, Bradley thought? I feel badly too.

Just because Bonnie was in the hospital in intensive care, she was getting all the attention.   It was me who ran to Mommy for help, thought Bradley.   Somebody should pay attention to me too.

Bradley fought with his anger and guilt. Throwing his toys at the wall, just didn't help at all. I don't like feeling guilty and I don't like feeling angry, thought Bradley, but what can I do?

Bradley just wanted to cry but crying made him feel even worse.

Later that night as Bradley lay in bed, his door opened. "Bradley are you still awake," asked his Dad?

"Yeah, I'm awake," Bradley sniffed.

"I'd like to talk to you about all of the things that have gone on the last few days.   May I come in and talk to you," asked Dad?

"Sure Dad, come on in," Bradley sniffed again.

Dad came in and sat on the edge of Bradley's bed.
"You can go and visit Bonnie tomorrow and let her know
how you are feeling."

Bradley looked at Dad and said, "What do you mean?"

"Well, son, I suspect that you have been feeling badly about all of this. Your sister is in the hospital. Maybe you are thinking you were at fault. Maybe you are even feeling angry that no one sees that you feel badly too," Dad said.   "I know this has been a hard time for you. It has been a hard time for all of us."

"You know even parents get scared and angry and feel guilty when something bad happens. I worked late the day Bonnie broke her leg. Maybe if I had been home earlier, she wouldn't have gotten hurt," Dad said.

Bradley was surprised. He never dreamed that maybe his parents were feeling some of the same things he was feeling.

Dad reached over and hugged him. "Bradley, we are all having a tough time but Mom and I love both you and your sister."

"Right now your sister is in the hospital and needs a little more attention than you do. We feel guilty that maybe we haven't paid enough attention to you.   You better believe though, that we love you and we haven't forgotten about you."

"Tomorrow we will go out and find a new stuffed animal for your sister. You can take it to the hospital and sur-prise her.   Maybe we can find a new toy for you too, for being so brave about all of this," said Dad.

Bradley hugged his Dad back and said, "Dad that is a great idea, I feel better now.   I love you and Mom. Soon Bonnie and I can play together again and everything will be back to normal. Good night Dad."

"Good night, Bradley, I love you," said Dad, as he turned off the light and closed the door.

Bradley sighed and fell asleep, feeling much, much better.

Other Books By Author William G. Bentrim

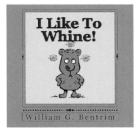

I Like To Whine is a series of scenarios of animals whining and the wise old owl gently chiding them and making suggestions as to why whining is inappropriate. At the end of the book there are some parenting strategies and activities for dealing with whining children. It is focused on elementary age children.
ISBN-10: 1442131721

Daddy Goes On A Trip addresses pre-school children and their concerns about parents who travel or are deployed. It is focused on elementary age children. At the end of the book there are some parenting strategies and activities for dealing with the stresses of military deployment and parental travel.
ISBN-10: 1449539734

Mommy's Black Eye is a children's book that addresses the complicated issue of domestic violence. It is focused on pre-school to middle school children. At the end of the book there are some parenting strategies and activities for dealing with this complicated issue. There are helpful contacts for those who find themselves in a domestic violence situation.
ISBN-10: 1449512577

The Adventures of Hardy Belch chronicle the exciting and unbelievable adventures of a normal 12 year old boy and his 240 pound telepathic dog. Hardy and Tiny (his best friend and dog) find themselves in many predicaments but as a team and best friends, they always end up helping others. Combining mystery and humor, each story is written to entertain and highlight the value of friendship, planning and selfless actions. ISBN-10:1449918530

"What About Me Resources"

The best article I found is provided by onconurse.com. I will summarize:

The emotional responses of siblings:

Concern	Fear	Jealousy	Guilt
Abandonment	Sadness	Anger	Worry

These emotions can lead to and be the cause of lethargy, general malaise, temper tantrums, acting out, unwillingness to go to school and with small children may lead to regression in areas like potty training.

Coping tools:

Make sure the child has a clear explanation for what their sibling is experiencing.

If the sick child is contagious, explain what that means, particularly to young children.

Use your digital camera to do photos and small recordings to go back and forth between the sick and well children.

Share your feelings about the situation.

Show empathy for the well child's feelings.

Schedule specific parent time with the well child.

If the sick child is hospitalized, take the well child for visits.

Give lots of demonstrative affection.

Alert teachers of the family situation.

The sick child will receive gifts, provide tokens to the well child for home or
school accomplishments and encourage the sick child to share.

Encourage grandparents, relatives or close friends to enhance their relationship with the well child if parents are frequently absent.

If your care facility has programs for sick and well children, take advantage of them.

<u>Additional Resources:</u>
Download the fact sheet summarized above for siblings of children with cancer. (PDF)
http://soundmedicine.iu.edu/segment.php4?seg=577
The Sibling Center at California Pacific Medical Center focuses on the needs of sick children's siblings.

Made in the USA
Monee, IL
21 April 2021